DID YOU KNOW?
Quokka

DID YOU KNOW?
Quokka
young
reed

Contents

What is a Quokka?

- Quokkas are **mammals**, so they are covered in **fur** and give birth to **live young** that feed on **mum's milk** in the first few months of life.

- They belong to the **marsupial** family, alongside animals such as Kangaroos, Koalas and Possums. After birth, young marsupials grow in their mother's **pouch**.

- Early European explorer's **mistakenly believed** that Quokkas were **large rats**!

Facts and figures

- Quokkas reach a maximum length of **fifty centimetres**, plus a **thirty-centimetre-long tail.**
- An adult can weigh up to **five kilograms.** When fully grown they are similar in size to a **large pet cat.**

The largest Quokkas grow to about the size of a large pet cat.

- Quokkas can live for about **ten years** in the wild or **fifteen years** in captivity.
- They are known for looking 'happy', but this is just because the **shape of their mouth** resembles a permanent smile.

Are these Quokkas smiling? No! It's just the shape of their mouths.

Getting around

- A Quokka's **hind-legs** are built for **power** and **speed**.
- Its **tail** acts as a **rudder** and helps to give **balance and direction** when hopping at speed.
- Surprisingly, Quokkas often **climb up into trees** in search of a leafy meal.

Note the strong back legs for hopping, and the tail that the Quokka uses like a rudder for balance.

Quokka climbing a tree.

Special adaptations

- The front paws are totally different from the back legs and feet, being much smaller and having **claws** to help with **feeding** and **grooming** the fur.

- Just like humans, Quokkas have sharp **incisor** teeth at the front for cutting their food and flat **molars** at the back for grinding it up.

Sharp front teeth help with cutting plant food.

The Quokka's front paws are designed for grabbing and holding food.

Quokka.

Small relatives of the Kangaroos and Wallabies, such as this Pademelon, are among the Quokka's closest relatives.

Closest relatives

- Within the marsupial family, Quokkas are included in a 'subfamily' called **macropods**. Macro means 'big' and pod means 'foot', so the name translates as **'big foot'**.
- The macropod family also includes larger animals such as **Wallabies** and **Kangaroos**, while some of the smaller relatives such as **Pademelons** are perhaps the ones that resemble the Quokka most closely.

In this image of a Quokka you can see its resemblance in shape to a Kangaroo or Wallaby.

Where do Quokkas live?

- Today Quokkas are known widely from **zoos and animal parks**, and also as a star attraction on the **internet** and **social media**, in the process becoming a favourite animal for millions of people.

Rottnest Island near the city of Perth is home to a population of thousands of Quokkas.

- In the wild, however, Quokkas live only in a few small areas of **woodland or scrub** in the south-west corner of **Western Australia**.
- On mainland Australia they have become very scarce due to the actions of humans, with the largest populations surviving on **offshore islands** such as Rottnest Island and Bald Island.

Quokkas are common on Rottnest and used to seeing many human visitors.

Life in the pouch

- Just like a young Kangaroo or Koala, a baby Quokka is known as a joey.
- At birth the joey crawls through mum's fur into her pouch. At this stage the one-centimetre-long baby is blind and has no fur – it looks like a small pink jelly-bean.
- As the young Quokka grows it emerges from the pouch to explore the world.

Larger joeys spend more and more time out of the pouch.

A Quokka joey in mum's pouch.

What's for dinner?

- Quokkas are **herbivores** – they mostly **graze on plants** such as grasses, flowers and leaves, particularly on the **tender new shoots**.
- They are mainly **nocturnal**, meaning that they are mostly active at night.
- Quokkas get most of their water from their food, so they **do not need to drink** very often.

Threats to Quokkas

- **Humans** are the main threat to Quokkas, due to the **deforestation** of their habitat and problems brought about by climate change, such as increased numbers of **bush fires.**

Bush fires can affect Quokka populations

- **Non-native predators** introduced by humans – such as **cats and foxes** – have caused many populations of Quokka on the Australian mainland to become **extinct**. Luckily **predator-free offshore islands** provide a **safe haven**.

- **Natural predators** of Quokkas include **Snakes, Monitor Lizards** and **Dingos**.

Offshore islands provide a safe haven from introduced predators such as cats

Dingos are among the native predators of Quokkas

First published in 2025 by New Holland Publishers

newhollandpublishers.com

A record of this book is held at the National Library of Australia.

ISBN 9781760798109

OTHER TITLES IN THE 'DID YOU KNOW?' SERIES:

Capybara
ISBN 9781760798048

Dolphins
ISBN 9781921078000

Kangaroos
ISBN 9781921073861

Koala
ISBN 9781921073878

Lizards
ISBN 9781921073885

Meerkat
ISBN 9781921073892

Penguins
ISBN 9781921073908

Otters
ISBN 9781760798093

Red Panda
ISBN 9781921073915

Sharks
ISBN 9781921078017

Tasmanian Devil
ISBN 9781760798055

For details of these books and hundreds of other Natural History titles see newhollandpublishers.com